The art of truth is pure
It is true love
From the heart
Hence Jamaican Art

It is picturesque
Pure gold
Heaven

It is you and me entwined
Blessed from above
Hence our true union written in the stars.

We are blessed by God – Good God hence we are
the truth in life – good life.

MICHELLE JEAN

Today I am broken and in need of healing
In need of a true friend
Need to be held by someone

Today I don't want to hear about God – Good
God. Just want to be me
Want to cry and be free
Want to lash out at God because today, I find no
truth in God and what he's told me about me.

Today, I find no truth in his love because to love
me so means nothing at all. To love me so
means just a tat hence not true.

All I have with God is failure and more failure
hence I am putting myself in the shoe of Eve
because I feel God has and have deceived me.

Lied to me about me and all he's given me.

My life is filled with pain but in all that pain, I
have yet to find someone to hold me and tell me
everything is going to be okay. I love you true.

All I have is music to heal me and it's a shame
that that music cannot be God himself being
beside me.

Yes I am broken hence this morning it's not No
Weapons by Fred Hammond that I hear, it's not

the voice of God that I hear, but Byron Cage's "Broken I'm Healed", that I hear.

We all need healing and lately I need it more than ever, but the one I need to heal me is not the one to do so.

Like I've said before, maybe I want and need God to be someone or something he cannot be.

I know God can speak, but yet he does not speak to me when I truly need him. All he gives me is music to heal me. Yes maybe this is his voice or way of saying I am there with you, and no matter your pain, your storm, I am still with you and I do truly love you.

He doesn't heal me when I need him to heal me. I know I have songs like these and he directs me to them but........I don't know. It's not the same.

Like I said, the road that I am on is rough and tough but to me this morning – well from last night, I think God is a liar. He's no different from Satan and the lie he told Eve (Evening) because there is no escape for me.

To me, what is given in the spiritual should be given in the physical. Meaning all the goodness God gives me in the spiritual, I need it in the physical as well. I don't know because I get so many beautiful things in the spiritual, but yet to receive them in the physical. Hence I am broken and without hope – faith in God – Good God on this day. Yes I truly love him but why can't I reach him when I need him. I mean why can't I just outstretch my hand and he just take it and squeeze my hand. Yes that would reassure me and yes I would want this every day but that's just me when it comes to him.

Today, I feel as if I am without truth the truth of God.

I feel as if he's a liar. And today I so do not want or need to make excuses for him because I am broken and I infinitely know him.

He's my guide and my true way but today I feel broken, as if he's not there with me or for me. I feel as if he's lied to me in all that he's given me in the spiritual realm.

I'm tried and tired.

Just want to live my life without God – Good God from now on. I don't want to even be in the same room or abode with him because I feel he's a liar and a thief because he's stolen my truth – my good life and true love.

You know when you are hurt and just need to have that person there to reach out to you and pull you into his or her arms and say its okay, I am with you. I am there for you. Well today this is where I'm at.

Today, I feel so much pain inside and in all that I do and complain to God he's not there to heal me. Right now I don't need songs. I need someone to hold me because I am but human that have true needs and wants.

I don't want to be on the road of God anymore because it's too painful. He's a liar because in all that he has given me, he cannot give me true peace and happiness. He cannot give me a good and clean life without the emotional pain and duress.

Yes I trust in what he's shown me, but I cannot trust him with my happiness, hence I am broken and cannot heal.

Truth is important to me and if what he's given me I cannot use in the physical, what good am I to him, me or anyone? Hence I feel as if I am on the losing side. Yes I want to escape but escape to where? I do not want or need to be on the side of death and I refuse to be. I do not need death; I need the truth and true love of God – Good God.

It makes no sense to me, if all I see is a lying system that causes pain.

It makes no sense to me, if I have to hurt so much and feel so much pain and the one that I truly love cannot save me from this hurt or pain. He makes me suffer continually because I find no happiness in him. Yes he completes me but where does truth and true happiness fit in with me and him? Where does happiness and truth fit in our complete system of things?

Where does unconditional love fit into all of this?

You cannot say as God you want truth and cleanliness when you as God cannot give absolute cleanliness and truth.

You cannot say you want us to love you when your love causes pain.

You cannot say you love us so when there is not truth in your love. You cannot you love is so when there is no truth in so.

Love us so can mean a tat.
Love us so can be a little bit.

Yes love us so can mean a lot. But I don't want so; I need true love and unconditional love of truth with you. So keep your love us so and give me your truth – true love of truth.

You cannot say you love us so and when tears come you have no one to help you ease your pain.

How can he God possibly know, when in your eyes he's not able capable to fulfill my needs?

Today it's good to say but what about doing?

I don't know if I am being ungrateful because I am hurt. But where is the truth in God when it comes to me?

Where's the truth in him when it comes to my hurt and pain?

Tell me, how can I be complete now when I am broken?

How can I be complete when God breaks me each and every day?

How can I be complete when I am emotionally drained?

Physically drained?
Financially drained?
Medically drained?

Emotionally wrecked?
Spiritually confused?

All this I feel but yet I am complete in some way.

Maybe I am confused.
Maybe depressed.

No, not depressed but stressed. Stressed out by children and the hardships that I have to face alone but I have to move on; hold on until my day comes when I don't have to worry about them.

Yes I look forward to the day when my spirit escapes the body and I don't have to deal with my children and the stress they give me anymore.

This prison that's called flesh and bones is keeping me from running away from it all. But one day I will be able to find the opening in my brain – head and truly escape from man and this world that I am living in.

I won't be dirty anymore.
I won't be living for God – Good God but living for me because I'll be truly free.

Yes the spirit seeks escape – freedom and one day, I will have it. And trust me, I won't go to

God's abode nor will I go to deaths abode. I will go to my universe that I've built for me excluding him.

A universe void of stress and pain
A universe void of God and Death
A universe void of inhumane people
A universe void of humans and spirit

A universe that is truly peaceful, harmonious, serene and truly happy

A universe that is truly happy and filled with pure happiness. Not the happiness of God – Good God because God – Good God does not make me happy.

A universe that is pure
A universe that can never die or grow old
A universe of pure truth and true love
A universe void of lies and untruth
A universe that has good and true light
A universe that heals and help

A universe that will grow up in goodness at all times

A universe that is not based on the lies of Sin and God – Good God but a universe based on absolute truth.

A universe void of all doubt and doubtful thoughts

A universe that has and have all the right and good answers and give it truthfully, harmoniously and peacefully at all times.

All that is good and true will be in this universe hence there will be no god or gods of any kind.

No death and sin of any kind.

Absolute truth will be the only one there with me because we will build in absolute truth, goodness and happiness at all times.

Yes, today I need my world and universe that is void of the pain of Death and God – Good God.

I need to be free and happy and the god that I am living for and with cannot give me happiness, hence there is no truth in him when it comes to the truth and happiness of man – humanity especially me.

One cannot give at all times. You will become burnt out. *Hence today I say unto man it is not better to give than to receive.* ***<u>The person that said it's better to give rather than receive is a damned liar and slave master.</u>*** *No one can give without receiving hence I too am* *a liar because I've said it's better to give than receive.*

No one can constantly give without getting. Hence this morning I truly ask for forgiveness when it comes to saying, it is better to give rather than to receive.

When you give constantly you will become broke and broken like me.

When you give constantly you will become mentally drained like me.

You become sick like me.

You become stressed and mentally unstable like me.

You become hurtful like me.

You become doubtful like me.

You become unloved like me.

You become alone like me.

You become spiritual and physically sinful like me.

So, **_know who you give your heart and true love to._**

Yes God says, he loves us so but loving us so, is not loving us true.

True love is what I seek and need. And if God cannot love me true, then in my world and book he is not worth it. Nor is he true because the word in the beginning was truth. It still is, **_hence truth is everlasting life. Truth created this universe and it is in truth that we must go back to the universe._** Like I've said, and will forever ever say. True love cannot hurt, so if I am hurting and I am telling God he's hurting me, can't make me happy, then something is truly wrong. **_I have to know when to walk away and live for me._** I have to truly love me and make me happy. But I do not need the restrictions of live – the restrictions of God. I cannot constantly write and give and get nothing in return.

And no, I do not write to get because I get true joy and peace from writing. Writing is my way of healing me. It's my way of communicating with me, the true me. It's my way of communicating with you and yes God to a certain degree.

Yes the world is filled with evil and pain but like I've told God, he too is at fault because in all he did, he did create evil and he must take responsibility for it. He must take responsibility for the evil he created which is negative energy.

Evil did not just come about hence life and death go hand in hand. Is from the hand of God. We cannot blame all on evil. At some point in life we have to take responsibility for our own actions and he God must do the same as well.

And no, this is not a contradiction of what I said in another book.

Every atom was designed to perform a specific function not just on earth but also in the spiritual realm.

Every particle was designed to perform a specific function in the lives of all in earth as well as in the spiritual realm.

Good and evil exist on earth and good and evil exist in the spiritual world. I do not need either of this abode. **_I need to find and be in the universe and world that is void of both realms – world. I do not need pain and hurt. I need truth and happiness, hence there has to be more to good life – truth._**

I cannot fight for the physical world and the spiritual world because both cause me hurt and pain. I have to leave both worlds behind because neither one of them is for me. Like I said, both worlds (physical and spiritual world) cause pain and hurt and I do not want or need anything to do with either of them. I'm the one feeling the pain hence I cannot trust God – Good God in either world.

Like I said, loving us so is not loving us true no matter how I mask my truth. Convince you and me of the "so".

God did not say he loved us TRUE. He said he loved us "SO". Hence I've told you the message said, "FOR GOD SO LOVE US HE IS WORTHY TO BE PRAISED." I've delivered his message and I question the validity of this message.

I've told you I've complained to God about this. He should not have to tell us he loves us so and that he is worthy to be praised. We are to know to thank him. We are to know that he is worthy. So for him to remind us of this, is simply wrong on his part.

He God wants praise, which is thanks. So to anyone that say it is better to give rather than to

receive, you are a damned liar because he God wants praise – thanks for what he has and have done for us.

So with all this said, who the hell won't be confused and find confusion in all that I have written. In all that I've written, I've found nothing which is something. I've found truth in me and in all that I do.

Thanks are something and when you do good unto someone, we are to get thanks in return. **_So it is not better to give than to receive. It is better to give and receive because the receiving that you get are YOUR BLESSINGS. A simple thank you is a blessing because that person is acknowledging that you did well – good unto them and they appreciate it._**

GOD – GOOD GOD REQUIRES THANKS SO WHY NOT MAN? Why should we not expect a simple thank you for the good that we have done?

Just to clarify myself before I go on. I said life and death go hand in hand and it is from God. God gave us life but when we sin we die hence life and death go hand in hand on earth as well as in the spiritual realm. Like I said, there is evil in both worlds and I do not want or need to be in either world. ***I need a universe and world that is void of the physical and spiritual. I need a true universe based and built on truth, absolute truth and happiness. I do not need the yoyo effect of either world. I need to be solid in truth as well as in me.***

My truth is not your truth nor is my world your world. God's world is not my world because I do not find absolute truth in God. Nor do I find it in the physical or spiritual world. ***<u>There is a greater universe yes. This universe is void of lies and pain – hurt and this is the place I need to be in. This universe is where I need to be.</u>***

<u>I also have to realize that guides are not gods.</u> They are just guides and they do lie to keep us satisfied – keep us going and I cannot have this anymore.

My life is not better with these guides in my life. My life is restricted because where I need to be I cannot get.

Yes, I will forever tell you what is shown to me in these books, but there comes a time when I will have to walk away just like the next man because to me, if God was true love he would not cause us so much pain.

I do not like hurt, nor do I like pain and I truly need truth and happiness and if God – Good God cannot truly make me happy why am I holding on?

I have to move on. I cannot let God hold me back from my happiness. No, I do not want to hurt him but if my decision causes him pain then so be it. He will know how I feel first hand. **_Emotionally I am hurting._** I am being drained and I am the one hurting myself and I can no longer hurt myself because of him (God). **_I have to live and I have to live void of sin. So if God is hurting me emotionally he too is causing me to sin and that is so not right. He's contributing to my hurt and pain – suffering, hence causing me to be ugly like sin._**

Yes everyone wants to be happy but how do we want to be happy?

What causes us happiness?

For some a simple thank you causes them happiness but is it true happiness?

Yes you may be saying. And that is great.

My god does not cause me true happiness because I seek and need true love from him and I cannot get it. Hence in my book and world God cannot love true. He can only love so and he's said it. He wrote it on the school wall. It said, "**_for God so_** love us he's worthy to be praised." "He loves us so", not "he loves us true". Yes I have a problem with this because so and true is not the same thing. As God and Good God you are to love us true. Hence today, I question the validity of God – Good God and his love for humanity and mankind. Yes me, especially me.

I am not questioning the existence of God because there is a God. The universe did not just come into being like that. Nor do particles collide as man would have us think. We see what our eyes want us to see, hence we tell lies because no one hath the eyes of God. Hence we cannot see God – Good God with our physical or spiritual eye in his true and original form. I cannot say, well water is life and it is life. Water is abundant in the physical and spiritual realm but water is not God. Hence water cannot be the true life of God. Water aids God hence we need it. But the true life and existence of God humanity does not know.

Water is one stage hence man knows not the makeup or truth of life – true life, that which is God – Good God.

We say the eyes are our window to the soul. True. Our eyes are the window to the soul, that which is the physical and spiritual as well as life and death. But true life hath no window hence we cannot see what we know not about. So because we know not God we cannot see him in his truest form.

Because we know not God we cannot be with him in his realm. Because all man – humanity know is life and death. The physical and spiritual, but beyond the realm of the physical and spiritual man do not know.

Maybe this is why I am not happy.
This is why I am alone.

Maybe this is why God does not make me happy because the world and life beyond the physical and spiritual I cannot explain. I know of the world beyond the physical and spiritual and this is my world of truth and happiness, but I cannot take you there because I know not how to get there on my own.

All I have is pain and confusion living in a shell – a prison that I want to rid myself of and can't.

Hence I tell you no one has to die to attain truth – true life with God – Good God. I do not want to die to go to a world where I have to suffer and live in pain all over again. Like I've said, spiritual pain is different from physical pain. Spiritual pain is more deadly. There is no mercy here and none is given once you are there.

Spiritual pain no one can handle.

No one lives in the spiritual world once you've accepted death in the physical world. You must die but before you die you have to feel pain. You have to suffer hence the poor man dies like the rich man and the rich man dies like the poor man.

Death is death in the grave. You cannot take your riches on earth with you to the grave. Hence the sufferings of the underworld – in the grave.

Death walks amongst the living and take the living with them (him and her) to hell. There are two types of death. Male Death. Male death kills by water but female death takes everything in her path. Her death is dry death. This is the best way I can explain it. When male death takes immediately or within three to nine months (3 – 9 months). Female death you cannot pinpoint because her death can take years. You cannot pinpoint her death because her time is not like male time, meaning the time of male death. She is the deadlier of the two. I've told you, when you can stop male death you cannot stop female death. Female death is the one to be scared of. And as messengers we fair her because she can take our lives if we piss her off. She does not like to be stopped. If you stop her once, watch out because she will put you on her docket if you stop her again. Even if you greet her in peace she will not return your greetings because she is pissed off at you. Every true messenger of God – Good God know this. Hence you have to know the colours of true death. That which is the African Unity Flag – the colour of the African Unity Flag that is. Those colours are the unification of death – DEATH UNITED.

And like I've said, there is no such thing as possessions meaning the dead cannot possess a person just like that. Infinitely and indefinitely impossible, so stop letting people fool you. If that person was not given to the dead or unto the dead, then no spirit can possess you. What belongs to the dead stays with the dead or with death. So if you have not given yourself unto death, then the dead and death cannot possess you. The dead is the dead whether it is physical or spiritual.

Well my child is possessed and I did not give my child over to death. You are crazy and infinitely wrong you are saying.

And I am telling you, you did. You gave your child over to death hence your child is possessed.

This is how it happens. If you are married to a physical demon then your child is possessed. There will be no peace for you in raising them. You have to be constantly praying and calling out to God – Good God for help like me.

There are no such things as physical demons you are saying.

I am telling you there are. These people are called fallen angels in your book of sin. **_There sole purpose in life is to take your life in the physical and spiritual. This I know for a fact hence I tell you to know your colours and your tree of life. Your tree of life and colours are significant in both realms, (the physical and spiritual)._**

Physical demons are the ones to come to earth and how you see them is in full black descending down on you – atop of you. **_These people are true demons. They have not life. They are your death in both worlds. Know this. What they do not finish in the living they will try and finish in death and this is why some of us die and can't figure out why we die._** If you have children with them the children will carry on tradition. Do all they can to stress you out so that you die. Like I said, this is where prayer, true prayer comes in because your prayer is constant like I've said.

Some of you are saying hell no, that is not true. Well hell yes it is the truth.

Suffering and pain is not just physical it is also spiritual hence you were told. **AS IT IS IN HEAVEN, SO IT IS ON EARTH.**

You have to know what you are dealing with.

When we accept death we are possessed. Meaning when you go to church and baptize your child, you are baptizing them unto death.

When your parents baptize you, they baptized you unto death, hence carrying on the tradition of death, sin and evil.

But but but.

There are no buts in life just truth. There are no buts in God – Good God's abode just water. Good clean and pure water. Water cleanses the spirit and it's the first to touch pure evil in the grave. ***Hence evil learns the truth of self and***

**see their ugliness – the ugliness of their sins in the grave.**

So once again, because we accept death we are possessed by demons – evil spirit, hence we do evil – sin.

God does not deal with blood he deals in water.

**Death deals in blood because blood is what he death must have before he can take you. He must drink blood hence he has you drinking blood. He has you sinning just so he can take you.**

You were told God does not deal in death only death deals in death. God is life – true life hence life cannot kill life only death can kill – take his own.

**Death cannot kill what belongs to God – Good God because all that belongs to God – Good God goes up and not down.**

Strayed but isn't that always me.

I start saying one thing and go off and leave you in the dust by talking about something else. Oh well I guess this is the true me. Confused as heck I think. Like I said, God does not make me happy and if he cannot make me happy here on earth, how is he going to make me happy when my spirit escapes the flesh?

If he cannot provide for me here on earth how can he provide for me in the spirit?

I will not settle for God is God nor will I settle for he loves us so because like I said, loving us so does not mean loving us true. I've tried to convince myself of this and I've even tried to convince you of this but something is missing in that equation.

You cannot say you love us so and cause us hurt and pain. Yes I've delivered your message Good God, but what about truth, the truth of you and me – true love? Can a man or woman love you so then turn around and hurt you? Deny you the truth – true love?

Can a man or woman say they love you so and leave you to die at the hands of wicked and evil people?

Yes, no weapons but what good are no weapons, when the one you truly love cannot love you true or unconditionally? They can only love you so. But yet, I can say I am complete. How does that work?

How does God – Good God complete me when at times I do not feel whole, I feel broken like today?

Yes, I have many questions and maybe I will never get the answers to what I am looking for because the answers that I seek, is already within me.

Who knows, maybe I am my worst enemy. But all I know is that, I am truly not happy. There is something missing. I know this and no matter how much I seek, I cannot find this something.

I know it's not God because I know how to reach him and even blast him at times. I've blasted him on many occasions you all know this. But why does happiness seem so important to me?

Why is cleanliness so important to me?
Why is sanity so important to me?

These things maybe trivial to some people but they are extremely important to me. Living a sin free life is extremely important to me, but yet I cannot have this here on earth. The sins of others do affect me, meaning the environment that I live in.

There is peace, true peace and this peace cannot be obtained in death, it can only be attained in life. Yet the road that leads me to this peace cannot be found and life cannot be found here on earth. Not in this present day and time, hence on days like these, I truly question the validity of God like I've said. And yes once again I have to separate guides from God because guides are not God because they do lie – mislead and this I cannot have.

Yes darkness surrounds me hence my spirit is like unto a Pit Bull like I've said. It is that intimidating – deadly. I see the ugliness of sins and my sin and that truly scares me.

But in all that I see I am not happy. Good God does not make me happy. I feel caged, trapped in a world that I so do not want to be in. I truly do not want to be in this land nor do I want or need to be around ugly people. Meaning sinful and wicked people. But where do I go to avoid this world of sin I truly do not know.

Many thing cause me pain and God – Good God is one of them because I still cannot comprehend why a God that say he loves us so would continue to allow us to live in sin.

Why would he continue to make us stressed and unhappy?

So now the question I ask? What is true love and why can I not find it?

If I've made God – Good God my true love, why can't he make me happy? Why can't he make me his true love unconditionally?

Why does he continue to make me live a sinful life in a world and country I truly do not want or need to be in?

Why does he keep me a prisoner in a world and country that I want to flee from?

Why did he truly allow sin and evil to make all on earth dirty – truly sinful?

Many questions I have but yet answers are none. Not even he Good God can give me the answers to the questions I am asking. So if God – Good God is willing and able, even capable, why are we the way we are? And why does sin have time to deceive and create havoc, when sin breaks all of his laws and rules including the laws and rules of sin?

So because sin has and have broken all the laws should sin not be destroyed?

I mean from the day sin broke the first law, should the time of sin not be null and void?

Should sin not have died long ago?

Should the lands and people of sin not be null and void? Meaning they sinned and uphold the laws and law of sin, so all the goodness of God – Good God should be taken from them. Good God should not let his goodness grow in the lands or countries of the dead – death.

No trees and water – food should they have because they did not choose him Good God, they chose death. So let death feed, clothe and provide water for them – his land and people. Come on now. Hence I say God – Good God upholds slackness and he's not truthful because he still feeds evil. He still maintains them, so tell me how can we be clean if God – Good God himself maintains slackness and lies – the children of the wicked and evil?

And no this has nothing to do with physical and spiritual time. Nor does this have anything to do with the rift in the space time continuum because man – humanity cannot define spiritual time. Humans – humanity cannot pinpoint a point or time in time hence we say a rift in time; space time continuum. There is time in time, hence spiritual time and physical time. Spiritual time being more advanced and ahead in time. So to say humans can tell time is a lie. Humans cannot tell time because if we could, time would not pass us by. We would be on the same time with time in time and at a point in time.

Confusing to you but simple to me because time cannot change nor is it constant. But we say constant because we do not know that time is life and without time there is no life – no anything. And like I said, in my other books we cannot have a void or darkness because that void or darkness is something. You can see that void or darkness, hence I tell you within the black hole there is light. Not because you cannot see it does not mean it's not there. Hence there is life – that life you cannot see with your natural and spiritual eye.

Yes I know, I need to talk more about the darkness so that you can comprehend it, but I can't because some darkness I cannot comprehend. Just know that there is physical and spiritual darkness. Spiritual darkness are our sins and I've told you they are ugly. ***So to say time, is to say life and since we cannot comprehend time, we cannot comprehend life. In order for us including me to see God – Good God in his natural state we, including me have to be void or rid of all our sins. We have to clean ourselves up properly and that is easier said than done because I do not truly know how to clean the spirit to make it clean. The cutting of the hair is one way but***

I do not know it this makes you truly clean. Because the sins against man is not the same as the sins against God – Good God.

To many, life hath to do with flesh but life hath nothing to do with flesh. It hath to do with energy and water in the spiritual and physical sense because without water we hath not life nor do we have time.

You know what let me leave this alone because I am going to get into something you know not about. Just know that everything is done in time at a point in time at the right time in time.

Yes this book is entitled Broken and this morning I am not so broken because I just got a twitter account. Something I did not want to do but I got anyway. Maybe now I don't have to write so much books. I can share with you my thoughts through twitter. Yes I wanted a My Space Account and hopefully one day I will end up on My Space. I will meet you on My Space in My Space.

Yes I still need a web page but I am waiting for the right people to make one for me. Infinitely need a web page. So for now enjoy me and remember I am not an exciting person. I am probably the most boringest person on the planet.

Yesterday, October 03, 2013 I was to broken, but after listening to Byron Cage I am okay. I also got a phone call yesterday from Jamaica and today I am so in the right mood. Like I've told you Jamaica is dirty and need cleaning. It's funny God – Good God told me Jamaica needed cleaning but he never told me how to clean it.

Suffice it to say, I dreamt I was with a family member and I got some Lysol not Pine Sol but Lysol and water and I was going to clean his place. So Jamaica get your Lysol. The yellow bottle with the liquid, yellow liquid and start cleaning Jamaica. Ammonia is also a yellow liquid and if you have that use that. Any yellow cleaning liquid start cleaning unnu house inside and out. Lysol was what I see so Lysol is the preferred cleaning aide. As for cleaning your spirit start juicing and start living clean. Jamaica can be saved, so it's up to you as a person now to start cleaning.

I guess God knew that I was going to complain about him not telling me how to clean up Jamaica when I got up. Trust me I did complain. I was complaining that he shows me these things but yet he never told me how to clean up Jamaica. We need to know how to clean not just house but self. ***He God cannot say we must live clean*** *without telling us how to make ourselves clean.*

A man or woman including child cannot say we are living for God – Good God and live in dirty lands. We're not clean but dirty.

I have to live clean. This is why I tell you I have to cut my hair because I did sin against God rude. Cutting my hair is my shame offering because your hair is your crown, your pot of silver and or white gold. Not yellow gold because yellow gold is discarded in the spiritual realm.

Yellow gold is your divorce papers in the spiritual realm. This is the best way I can describe it for you to understand.

So yellow gold have no worth in the eyes and sight of God – Good God in the spiritual world.

So when anyone tell me they are going to walk the streets of gold in heaven, I have to say which heaven? No human being can tell you what the abode of God – Good God look like. No dirty person or spirit can enter the kingdom and abode of God – Good God. We say heaven is where God – Good God resides and I say stop lying on God – Good God because no one knows where Good God reside, not even me. I am not perfect meaning clean enough, but one day I will. And like I said, if the Crystal City is where Good God resides, then yes I want to go there because the beauty of the outside is more than a sight to behold. If the outside is that beautiful can you imagine the inside?

So broken am I, but soon everything will be okay with me. I know the truth of life, hence I know the full truth of Good God and although I cannot see him, I know he's with me and in me.

I am but a human vessel that hath life – energy and although that energy is tainted by blood I will one day become clean. I will shed the blood that is within me and live clean in time with time. I will have his good and pure water to surrounds me, clean me, live with me as well as sustains me.

I am broken in spirit but never broken in truth – true and good life.

Many questions have I but that's me. The truth and goodness of Good God is within me.

I am pure at heart hence the truth is pure and good within me and around me.

I am dark but though the darkness I can see the light, that which is the mountain and truth of

God – Good God. The truth is within me hence at times I am broken – cannot see.

Broken am I because I am living in a world plagued with violence and crime.

Broken because human dignity means nothing to some – the elite and governments of society – this sinful world.

Broken because the truth no longer resides with man – humanity. He's left us to fend for self – our own, hence we live like dogs begging for a bone.

Broken because man – humanity have and has made self unworthy of truth and good life – Good God – Time.

Broken because man hath no true love. Hence we live as thieves vying for a place in the Babylonian thieving system of corruption and deceit – sin.

Broken because life has no worth. And grown ass men and women prey on the innocent of society making them victims to their world of wreck – wrecking ball of sin and death.

Broken because the black race and nations have left God – Good God. Hence Good God cannot trust us because we gave him up for the devil's own. Babylonian gods of death and torment –

true and living demons that plague the earth and spiritual world.

Broken because man knoweth not the truth of life hence they cannot live by truth. Nor can they live in time with time or on time. They can only live by lies, their lies and deceit – sins.

Broken because man is slated to die before 2032 and no one is doing a thing to save self – humanity.

Broken because we over eat and over produce by chemical means and not by organic means.

Broken because we've polluted the earth beyond repair – good will – good life.

Broken because we cannot see self nor can we see the goodness of Good God.

Broken because all that you read in these books many will continue on their evil path saying, I am a liar and one will save them in the grave.

<u>But I say unto you that will reject me and Good God, you are the deceived because there is no life in death and no one can live beyond the grave.</u> No one will have life after death because when you are dead you are dead and God – Good God does not deal in death, he deals in life. And without good life you cannot see Good God nor will you be able to reside with him.

You are the deceived because heaven is not the home or abode of Good God.

You are the deceived because if you are not living clean, you are living as the dead of hell. Hence you are the walking and living dead.

Yes we all sin but with forgiveness and remission of sin, you cannot live you must die. You must go down to hell and die with sin and death. Satan and his deceiving crew.

You are the deceived because the life you live in the living, determines where you go in the afterlife – hell.

You are the deceived because a man cannot clean the flesh without cleaning the spirit.

Yes I am broken but there are many broken me's out there.

Many broken spirits
Many broken homes
Many broken children
Many broken lives
Many broken parents

And in all that we do to fix we end up destroying.

We destroy our children
Our marriage
Our sanity
Our life
Our home
Our business
We destroy self including the god that we say we love.

We have become deceivers
Backbiters
Demons
The children of vanity – egos
The children of death

All this we've become but yet we've all forgotten that ***the wages of sin is death*** – we die in time.

We grow old due to sin and nothing else.

Yes some can and will argue environmental allergens, but I say onto you, environmental allergens are a cop out for many because our sins do affect the environment we live in. Hence we live to kill. Built to eliminate and destroy.

The next man's sins affect me and you because sins are dirty and the more we sin

the dirtier we get, the uglier our spirit become.

Yes I am broken, tried and tested but am I that broken. I say not. I am healed but not that healed because whether we like it or not tomorrow does come. It just turns into today – the next day.

Yes I need you just as you need me, hence we are not truly broken because no one can glue the broken pieces of the spirit with crazy glue.

We are but confused, delusional at times. But never broken because no one can break the spirit hence energy cannot be broken or separated from life – good life.

No one can break water.
No one can alter water.
No one can create water.
No one can sustain or maintain water.

Hence we cannot maintain the spirit because we know not the source of ALL.

We say we know, but if we know, we would know all that is spiritual also.

So beyond the realm of the physical and spiritual lies true life; the source of all. It is energy, it is water; it is true time.

This time is not constant because life is not constant. Life is truth hence there is truth in true time.

There's a time for everything, but in truth there is a time for nothing at all. But does all have time? I say not. Because not all have life – good life. **_The time of death is not true time but a point in time – his time for him to die alongside his own. Each life he takes (death takes) he dies alongside you._** Everyone dies in time at a point in time, hence the death of man is not today but at a point in time – spiritual time. The time when physical time catches up to spiritual time.

Weird to you but like I said, I know time hence the time of man is not the same as the time of God – Good God. Because in time there is no time just life – true and good living. Pure harmony and truth living side by side in a different world – dimension that is not known to man.

Yes you may think me weird, but I am not waiting on the plane of man but the plane of God – Good God.

With him there is true flight. Hence the realm of God is not the realm of Man. Nor is it the spiritual realm.

Here lies my spirit. See it if you can.

Wash it
Clean it if you dare

I am but human
Flesh that stinks
Flesh that is the prison of my spirit

Yes I see to discover
Travel beyond the realm of man
But within these prison walls, I find insanity
Control
Dominion
Puss
Lack of truth
This is the body hence we are dirty
Of the earth
Earthly

I am spirit but that spirit has become dirty
I've become like man
Vain
Lustful
Sinful
Dirty
Dead

I am not a clean vessel anymore because I do the
things of man – humanity.

I procreate like demons do.
Lay with males
Some with females

We marry into sin
Have children for sin

We've forgotten goodness. Hence we do not have
children in goodness, we have them in sin.

Yes I am you and you are me.
I am human
That of flesh and bones
That which was born in prison – flesh and bones

So behind these prison walls I look
I cannot see me
I cannot see my reflection within

I am but lonely
Rail and paper thin

I am fat
Huge
Tall
Short

I am divided

A Pit Bull
Even a Mack Truck

I am your mother
Your sister
Your wife
Your brother

I am human
Your cousin
Your alternative life
Significant other

I have a voice but evil tries to shut me up
We are being controlled

Are controlled because religion dictates all that
you do. We do.

You have no voice or say because you are silent
You are a part of the collective of sin
The devil's world – domain

You buy sin hence you live in sin
You lie for sin
Do all for sin including die in sin

I am me
Trying to be free

I am a writer

Your lover
Your flavour and favour

I am the cherry in your chocolate tea
The honey if you don't favour cherry

I am your bed
The one you ride including the one you sleep in

I am your joy
Your boredom

I am your egg
Your sperm

I am your child
I am all that you need me to be including your
good and perverted thoughts.

I am your underwear
Your skirt but never your pants.
I am your ice cream
Your yogurt
Bath oil

I am you because you are me
I am freedom
Free spirit
Freedom of thought

I am freedom of expression

Hence I walk nude in my own home when the spirit wants me to.

I bathe nude never with my clothes on
I wash myself hence washing my spirit

I bathe in freedom because no one can tell me how to bathe me.

I dress in freedom because my way of dress is certainly not your way.

I have sex freely, well not anymore because I do not have that right someone in my life yet. But if I did, he would have to know how to do me. He wouldn't be broken nor would he be able to cheat or break me.

Fidelity is rare but golden. Sex is not an everyday thing, it's just for those rare occasions. See it's a spiritual thing because spiritual sex is so much better than the real thing – physical thing. So yes, sex is the way I want it, how I want it and when I want it. No sorry need it.

So yes, when I have him I will have sex freely the way I need it to be. No limits or restrictions because the spirit needs sex, hence it is good for the body – soul.

Yes I will have him and if I want to tie him to a tree and do him. I will do it because he's mine and no one can tell me how to do him, except for God – Good God.

My sex life is my sex life. It does not involve you, or him (the man next door). It involves me and my blessed union. The perfect and true someone God – Good God has given me. So mind your own damned business and don't tell me how to have sex or make love in my own home. I am not married or committed to you I am married and or committed to him her. My way is not your way, so stay having sex your way and let me truly make love my way which is Good God's true way. He does not restrict me from having it all over time, so why should you?

Not because your sex life is boring it does not mean mine should be.

Not because your sex life is perfunctory, it does not mean mine should be. I want to take him beyond the bed post and have him in a tree. That's my way not yours, so truly leave me be.

Yes the roof top is fun if I can do him on the roof – our roof not a roof for public display.

Yes there are days when I will be boring but on those exciting days, the champagne will come into play. I have my cup and you have your straw. You get me. Truly hope you know what I mean. If you don't know or get it, let the picture on the first page entice you, talk to you. Now I hope you get what I mean, get me because honey I truly get you. Will receive you too.

Yes I'll roast him and barbeque him because nuts I like and he's got a good pair of sack – well basket balls. So yes baby I do play hence the brief thing cannot do.

Boxers yes, never briefs
Need him hanging for the days I take sorry play

Yes the floor will do so don't tell me what I can and cannot do with him. He's married to me, committed to me and I am to him.

So on this day, to all that say sex is this and sex is that. Don't restrict me because God – Good God does not restrict truth nor does he restrict true and clean loving – sex. If he did, you would not come about. We are the ones to marry true demons. So truly leave me and my bedroom alone because honey is mine and I am not afraid to do him. But will never share him. Fidelity remember.

Michelle Jean

Yes I thought I was broken but I am holding on.

I have to live
Have to be true to me

So to all of you, have a coffee with me?
Go get a cup and let's be one together.

Okay Kay, I know you don't like coffee but a tea will do. So get your favorite tea, drink it and truly think of me. No bad thoughts good thoughts only.

"Oh forgive me. How was your day?"

"Did you have fun at work?"

"No."

"Okay let's do something different together. I need to unwind you."

"Are you in bed?" Oh man I so do not want to spoil the mood, but if you are not in bed go into your bed for me because you are Kay too.

Once again.

"Are you in bed?"

"Yes"

"Do you have your tea?"

"Yes"

"Put it on the night table or night stand for me."

Find this CD for me.

JUST TO BE CLOSE TO YOU BY THE COMMODORES.

"Don't have it?"

"No."

"Go to YouTube and upload it."

"Have it?"

"Yes."

"Now let me share me with you because you are my girl, my man, my lover, my true love; my everything including my hope and faith and good song."

Come on let's do it. Get up off the bed.

"Do you have a picture of me?"

"No."

Well think of me. Use the picture on my twitter. Hopefully I'll get a better one with not so much gray hair.

Take my hand because I've found you.

Ah that feels so good. Your hand is warm and tender.

Put your arms around me but before you do, may I have this dance?

"This is more than our moment. This is our lifetime together because I more than need you. You are my lifetime of love and truth and you are whom I need next to me forever ever. So no matter your bad day you are my good joy."

You are my true love and lover for all time.

Enjoy me like I enjoy you.

Come a little closer.

Bury your head in my shoulder as I kiss you atop your head and on your cheek too.

Always remember I love you true.

"How do you feel in my arms?"

"Good."

"I'm glad because I am so not done."

Take this bracelet of truth from me. It's green so wear it always in truth of me. It's made with beads – green beads from the Kingdom of Kenya. It signifies truth, our truth. Never forget my true love of you.

Continue to hold my hand. Stay there while I look at your beauty.

Valentine's Day they are for lovers that are true and because you are my Valentine each and every day, I have this song especially for you. Listen carefully because this song I dedicate to you.

R. Kelly's HEAVEN CHOSE YOU.

You are my heaven because heaven did send me you. You are my forever ever true love and as I touch you, make love to you, you are my night and day – everything that is good. So darling, hold on to me because I truly don't want or need to let go of you.

You are my forever ever.
My truth
My blessing
My good angel sent by Good God
You are my right hand of God – Good God.

You are my good life and as long as I have the breath of life, I will always cherish you because God – Good God sent me you and I more than truly love you infinitely.

Michelle Jean

Yes I am so in a different mood today and it is this mood of truth and true love that I need each and every day.

I need to heal and it is with songs like these I find strength and hope.

It is with songs like these I can connect with you. So to all the Kay's of my world and kingdom – universe, hold on with me and know that Good God chose all of you for me.

We are in this together hence we are strong.
We are united
We are a good and true family and this is how I need us to stay forever ever infinitely.

We cannot be divided because if we are divided, we will become weak and lose faith. And I so don't want or need us to be that way.

If I have one apple or mango all of us must share that one apple or mango together.

IF I AM IN A RACE WITH YOU, ALL OF US MUST CROSS THE FINISH LINE TOGETHER. I REFUSE TO WIN THE RACE BY MYSELF. I MUST WIN IT WITH YOU. WE MUST FINISH TOGETHER AT THE SAME TIME.

In this relationship, there are no you be the winner in all. We must be the winner in all that we do. That means if I have a pie you must share that pie with me. This is how I need things to be.

We may not always have good days, but when I am weak you must be strong for me and when you are weak I must be strong for you.

If you are in pain, I must be there putting the water bottle on your tummy and rubbing your head, telling you that everything is going to be okay.

If you are ill, I must be the one praying and sending up good prayers for you and telling God – Good God to let things be okay with you. I should be able to come to you and visit with you to make you feel better even if it's for a minute or two.

Certain lands I know I cannot come in, but I am hoping one day Good God will make it possible for me to visit you – see you. I know there is Skype. So trust me we will be okay.

So on this day as I look in your eyes, I give you my truth and tell you that everything will be okay. The rough weather is just for a little while, but we will get through this together.

We are strong and not weak.

In truth and true love there are no sacrifices to be made, hence we will work together to pay our bills.

We will work together in getting through your sickness.

We will work together to stay sane.

Your tears I will dry and even cry with you because in all that I do, I do in truth not just for me but for you also.

I will not make you die in vain. I give you my word that I will hold on to you. I will not let death have you or take you to hell because my goodness is your goodness as well. This I give you my word on, hence you share in the goodness I do and Good God knows this.

I cannot see the mountain and leave you behind. You have to be on that mountain of goodness with me. This is what a true family is all about.

We work together in unison to get to the top and see Good God.

I need you and you need me hence we need each other.

Know that in our midst Good God must be there. He must be in the middle, the front, back and sides of it all.

I cannot do this alone.
I cannot live alone.
I cannot write alone.
I cannot ride and fly alone.

I need you to be there with me, just as how I need Good God to be with us at all times.

So in all that we do, let's hold on together and get to the finish line together.

I will not overtake you because I don't believe in overtaking. We are together hence together we must stand.

Together we must be forever ever because time hath no end for the goodness and righteous and we are goodness and righteousness.

We will be in time and be time because we are true – free.

Michelle Jean

I will stand with you through your pain and ordeal.

I will be the one sitting by your bedside saying darling I love you true.

I will be the one holding your hand and giving you strength on the days you are weak.

I will be your feet when you cannot move – walk no more.

I will be your joy when you cannot take the pain no more.

I will be your reader of poetry.
I will even write them for you too.

No, no, not sing because Good God did not bless me with the melody of songs – tunes.

I will be your rain on a hot day.
I will cool you down my way.

I will be the wind that drives your clouds away.
I will be all that you need me to be as long as all you need is goodness and truth.

Michelle Jean

My darling, I cannot change me, meaning what I've done in the past. But I can change the way I do things when it comes to truly loving you.

See I did not know what I had
Did not treat you right
Did not appreciate you

You've been my life time and life line
You've been with me through my ups and downs. And although I cannot change time or go back in time, I can change the way I love you.

I can no longer love you wrong
I have to love you right
I have to love you in truth
Give you truth

I am a different person now.
I don't want to hurt us anymore.
I am not alone in this, you're in this with me

I know I did you wrong and I am truly sorry for hurting you. I cannot undo what I've done, but I can be the better person I need me to be – you need me to be.

There are no lies in truth
There are no cheating in truth
No extra marital affairs in truth
No exam to pass in truth

No kingdom to dominate or kill for

All there is in truth is truth – true love and I do truly love you.

My past is not the greatest with you, but we can make a better future together. Will you please forgive me?

Will you please forgive me for the pain I've caused you?

Will you please forgive me for the shame I've caused you?

See life does not come with instruction manuals and we do mess up. We do make mistakes, but I wasn't man enough, woman enough to own up to my wrongs, and I am hoping it's not too late for us. I cannot promise you that I won't mess up from time to time, but on the days I mess up, will you continue to be there for me, hold on to me?

I will not say it's because I am human that I mess up because if I said this, I will be giving you excuses and I am not into excuses today or ever will be.

What I know is that you are the right one for me. You are the right queen and king for me.

You are the right heaven and paradise for me and I truly do not want to lose you.

Without you I'm lost.
Like a plane without wings
A ship without its sail

You are my captain, hence I give you my word that I will not sink our boat.

When there is no breeze, I will be the breeze that drift us along smoothly.

I will be that light gust of wind that gets us to our final destination.

You are my hope
My need and I truly love you.

Michelle Jean

I so do not want to end this book but I have to.

Wow.

It's Friday October 04, 2013 and I have to say good bye. Not good bye in that way because I truly need you.

You are my amazing days and thoughts so as I leave you.

I leave you with LOVE YOU FOREVER by Konshens.

I also leave you with UNCONDITIONAL LOVE by Jah Cure.

It is my hope that one day you will see the unconditional love I have for you and you and you.

So truly embrace me because we need to keep each other warm. I truly need to be close to you as the Commodores said. It's no joke, but my real world. Hence you are in my world of truth and true love with me.

Michelle Jean